For

SUELLEN

FROM: AUNTIE
1998

A Cup of Herbal Tea

By Beth Mende Conny

Illustrated by Jo Gershman

Designed by Arlene Greco

Peter Pauper Press, Inc.
WHITE PLAINS, NEW YORK

Notice: Herbs are powerful healing agents, and can be harmful if misused. This book gives very general, anecdotal advice, and is not a medical reference book. Before trying any herbal tea or recipe, first sample a small quantity in case you have a negative or allergic reaction. Do not self-treat for any long-standing problem without consulting a qualified medical herbalist, and check with your doctor before using herbs if you are being treated for any medical problem.

Dessert recipes prepared by Barbara Bloch

For Aunt Mollie, with love

Copyright © 1997
Peter Pauper Press, Inc.
202 Mamaroneck Avenue
White Plains, NY 10601
All rights reserved
ISBN 0-88088-065-1
Printed in China
7 6 5 4 3 2 1

Contents

Introduction

In the Beginning

Brewing the Perfect Cup of Tea

Herbal Healing

Growing Herbs

Harvesting the Rewards

Dessert Recipes to Accompany Herbal Teas

Our Personal Tea Ceremony

The Visual Beauty of Herbal Tea

Introduction

As the sun comes up, I like to settle down with my morning companion—a piping mug of herbal tea. I love the warmth of the mug against my cheek and the rich scents—chamomile, peppermint, rosehips, hibiscus—that rise in the air.

This, I think, is life as it should be: calm, soothing.

I also think about how herbal teas capture life's natural richness

in a single cup. Their many flavors excite my taste buds and imagination, and transport me to far-off corners of the world, where their ingredients grow in bountiful fields and atop majestic mountains. To think that a mere drink can be so exotic and basic!

Journey with me then and explore the world of herbal teas. Together we'll discover what ancient kings, philosophers, and peoples have known and enjoyed over the centuries.

B. M. C.

In the Beginning

*E*mperor Shen Nung, who ruled China in 2737 B.C., observed that those who boiled their water tended to be healthier than others. Wanting to ensure his own good health, he advised his servants to do the same for him.

One day, while he was visiting a neighboring province, a breeze blew some leaves into the Emperor's boiling pot of water. As the leaves steeped, they released a fragrant smell that enticed him to sample the brew. He was so taken with the taste

that he had his servants cultivate the plant in his garden.

And thus began the tea-drinking tradition that would pass from generation to generation, continent to continent.

When the Pilgrims journeyed to the New World in 1620, they

brought the best of the Old World with them: the seeds and plants of their favorite herbs.

Once ashore, they discovered yet other herbs that could be picked from the wild or cultivated to make great-tasting teas and cures. Chamomile, peppermint, and elderflowers–all found their way into the piping pots of tea so commonplace in Colonial days.

Herbal teas were especially popular during the Revolutionary War, when patriotic souls shunned imported teas in favor of those

that were home grown. One particular brew—made from sage, rosemary, mint, and balm—was called, quite aptly, Liberty Tea. Another, introduced by the Indians, was called Oswego Tea and was made from bergamot flowers.

With their hard-fought independence, Americans became less dependent on herbal teas. Black teas, imported directly from China, became more accessible and less expensive. Coffee consumption was on the rise

as well. Nevertheless, herbal teas kept their place in the hearts, diets, and medicine cabinets of Early Americans. That place has grown once again, as we and other enthusiasts rediscover the joys and benefits of herbal teas.

Brewing the Perfect Cup of Tea

*H*ow do you brew the perfect cup of herbal tea? Why it's all in the wrist—and the taste buds, nose, and eyes!

Some herbs like hibiscus and rosehips take mere seconds to release their tangy, aromatic flavors. Others like chamomile and lavender take several minutes or more before their unique qualities can best be appreciated.

Much, of course, depends on the tea we're steeping and how it is

being steeped. Much also depends on our personal preferences. No two herbs are alike, after all. To reach perfection, we must use taste, color, smell, and even previous brewing experience as our guides.

Like many great endeavors, tea brewing requires the proper tools. Not all necessarily used at once, these include:

A great-tasting tea–Thanks to the ever-growing popularity of herbal teas, many fine teas and tea blends are now available in local supermarkets and health food stores. All come with directions for steeping. Add hot water, a bit of wrist action, and you're all set.

An infuser–Used to make single cups of tea from loose herbs, infusers are spherical little suitcases covered with pin holes that hold the tea as it steeps. General rule of thumb: 1 teaspoon of dried herbs or 3 teaspoons of fresh herbs for each cup of tea.

A pot for boiling water–Stainless steel pots are ideal; enamel pots are also good to use, as long as they aren't chipped. Avoid tin and aluminum pots because they can add a metallic taste to the water.

A teapot for steeping and serving loose or bagged tea– China and earthenware pots make a particularly nice presentation for company; they also make solo tea-drinking more festive. Silver pots are nice as well, but they're expensive and difficult to keep clean.

A strainer to catch loose tea leaves–For teas steeped in a

teapot, simply hold the strainer over the cup before pouring. Some teapots have strainers already built into their spouts; others have a deep ceramic strainer that sits within the lid's opening.

The right water–Believe it or not, water has a taste that can affect the subtle flavor of a tea. If tap water isn't up to snuff, consider using bottled water. Further, always use fresh, cold water. Bring it to a full boil and use it immediately. Water that boils for an extended period of time can leave some teas tasting flat.

A favorite mug (or two or three)–We have our favorite herbal teas, so why not our favorite mugs? Let's choose those that match our needs and moods–giant ceramic mugs to warm our hands on cold winter mornings, delicate china cups to enjoy light-tasting after-dinner brews, clear glass mugs to delight in the vivid yellows, reds, ambers, and greens of chamomile, rose-hips, chicory, mint . . .

Herbal Healing

*A*ncient Romans boasted that they had no need for doctors. Instead, they relied on herbs like sage and thyme, rosemary and fennel, to cure their ills.

Today, we, too, can embrace the wisdom of the ancients. Herbal teas can help ease our aches and pains, aid our digestion and sleep, cleanse our systems, and cheer our hearts and minds.

Many of us have read of the benefits of chamomile and ginseng. Now, however, we're discovering

the beneficial qualities of scores of other herbs. Some, we're learning, can be used as an alternative or supplement to traditional medicine, particularly for minor ailments like colds, sore throats, and stress. True, we know it's best to consult a health professional when ill, and that some herbs, when taken in excess, may do more harm than good. Nevertheless, it's good to know that herbal teas can help us more actively promote our health and well-being.

Selected herbal teas—their unique qualities and reputed medicinal value:

Agrimony
A favorite tea in France, agrimony makes a good black-tea substitute and has an apricot-like flavor that goes particularly well with honey and licorice. It is said to regulate the bowel, strengthen the liver, and ease indigestion and urinary disorders. It is also used as a gargle for sore throats and laryngitis.

Angelica
Once believed to have the power

of angels, angelica is said to relieve colds, coughs, and fevers, and to combat colic, flatulence, and rheumatic inflammations. Its taste is similar to that of Chinese black teas, with a slight celery flavor. For a nice twist, blend it with juniper berries.

Anise
Also called aniseweed, anise was one of the first herbs brought to America, where it is widely used to flavor candies and liqueurs. Its great licorice-like taste makes it a good complement to other herbs and shortbread cookies. It can also

be added to hot milk for a wonderfully soothing before-bed drink. Anise is said to relieve asthma, bronchitis, colic, and nausea, and to promote sleep and lactation.

Bergamot
Also called bee balm, bergamot is an American wildflower that has a minty flavor when steeped. Used extensively today as an aromatic antiseptic, it may perhaps relieve nausea and flatulence.

Blackberry
Blackberry makes a full-bodied,

tangy tea, especially when blended with herbs like strawberry. Usually sweetened with honey, it is said to relieve inflammation, intestinal disorders, and anemia, and to freshen the breath. Blackberry may also be added to wines or brandies.

Chamomile
Chamomile is one of the oldest and most widely used herbs. Its delicate, apple-like taste makes it a wonderful follow-up to a big meal. Chamomile also makes a great addition to minty blends. For an interesting twist, brew it with hibiscus or dill seed. Long

renowned for its medicinal qualities, it is said to relieve anxiety, insomnia, indigestion, fever, sore throats, and colic.

Ginseng

Although bland in flavor, ginseng has long been revered, not so much as a tea but as a reputed cure-all that increases sexual potency and body strength, lengthens life span, lifts depression, lowers blood pressure, and produces a sense of well-being. It is best served sweetened with sugar or honey, and may be blended with licorice and other herbs to give it a lift.

Hibiscus

A popular ingredient in African, Far Eastern, and Caribbean foods, hibiscus has a tart, lemony flavor that blends well with herbs like chamomile. For a spicy, lemony flavor, mix it with rosehips and lemon verbena. Hibiscus is rich in calcium and iron, and is said to relieve stomach problems, increase sexual potency, and calm the nerves. It is also used to sweeten the breath.

Juniper Berries

Used commercially to make gin, fragrant juniper berries have a

spicy taste that nicely complements angelica. Juniper berries are said to relieve inflammation, cramps, digestive problems, and gastrointestinal infections, to be useful as a diuretic, and to ease rheumatism and arthritis.

Lavender
A beautiful herb with culinary and cosmetic uses, lavender has a strong aromatic smell and taste. Some recommend that it be blended with other herbs, such as equal parts of spearmint, cloves, rosemary, and lemon balm. On its own, lavender is

said to treat insomnia, nervousness, heart palpitations, halitosis, gas, and dizziness, and to stem depression and headaches.

Lemon Verbena
Native to Peru and Chile, lemon verbena has a refreshing lemony flavor that makes a nice addition to black teas and herbal blends that include rosehips and hibiscus. It also makes a wonderful accompaniment to lemon-flavored desserts. Lemon verbena is said to lessen melancholy, and to relieve colic, cramps, asthma, migraines, and toothaches.

Licorice

A great thirst-quencher with a distinctively sweet taste, licorice is said by some to help smokers quit without weight gain. It blends wonderfully with other herbs, including agrimony, and is said to relieve bronchial and stomach problems, coughs, congestion, ulcers, and bladder and kidney difficulties. It may also ease menopausal changes.

Mint

Varieties of mint, including spearmint and peppermint, abound, some 30 in all. Known and loved for their cool, menthol flavor, they make for a refreshing cup of hot or cold tea, and as a nice complement to vanilla ice cream and wafer cookies. Mints also work wonderfully when blended with other herbs. Try, for example, mixing spearmint, rosehips, chamomile, lemon verbena, and a twist of orange peel. Mint teas are said to relieve cramps, coughs, digestion, nausea, heartburn, abdominal pain, and headaches, and to promote calmness.

Raspberry

Soothing, fruity, and highly aromatic, raspberry is somewhat astringent and should be served with honey or sugar. Nevertheless, it makes a great addition to blended teas and adds zip to black teas. It is said to relieve morning sickness and ease childbirth, and to relieve diarrhea, bleeding gums, and sore throats.

Rosehips

Rosehips matches the orange as a source of Vitamin C, and is also high in vitamins A, B, E, and K.

Often blended with hibiscus, it makes a great wake-up tea and a delicate accompaniment to morning croissants and muffins. The herb is said to ease stomach disorders and female ailments, to fortify the heart and brain, and to combat colds and exhaustion.

Sarsaparilla
Enjoyed for its root beer/licorice-like flavor, sarsaparilla makes for a refreshing and fragrant tea. It is believed to relieve ulcers and wounds, promote tissue growth, and help psoriasis and other skin conditions.

Strawberry

A rich source of vitamin C, strawberry makes for a delicious, berry-like tea, especially when blended with other herbs. It also may be added to wines or brandies. Strawberry is said to relieve anemia, menstrual irregularities, diarrhea, and jaundice, to prevent excessive sweating, and to stimulate the appetite.

Valerian

Found throughout the world, valerian is said to be one of the most useful herbs in calming the nerves and strengthening the immune system. It also is believed

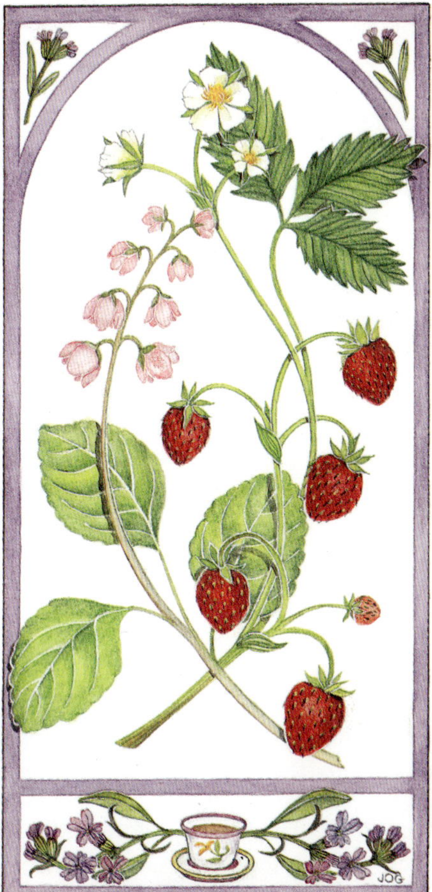
JOG

to relieve migraines, insomnia, and vertigo, as well as cramps and colic. Because of its somewhat bitter taste and odor, it should be sweetened with sugar or honey, flavored with spices like mace, or blended with other herbs.

Wintergreen

Cool, crisp, and minty, wintergreen is a favorite flavoring agent and is commonly used in homemade root beer. Like other mint teas, it is refreshing served either hot or cold. Wintergreen, it is said, may be used to treat colds, fevers, headaches, rheumatism, and aches and pains.

Growing Herbs

*T*hanks to the ever-growing popularity of herbal teas, we can get the most popular varieties at our local supermarkets and health food stores. So why grow our own?

Granted, growing herbs is not for all of us, and it requires work. But it's also fun and a great way to create our own blends. Better yet, we get to enjoy our favorite herbs "fresh off the vine," when their color, fragrance, and taste are at their peak. And here's the best news of all–herbs grow as easily indoors as they do out. So whether we have a large garden plot or a single ceramic pot, we're in business!

All herbs thrive in a soil that's well drained, nutrient-rich, and pH-balanced. For best results, try an equal mix of soil, peat moss, sand, and perlite.

When planting more than one herb, label pots or rows. (It's surprising how many seedlings look alike!) It's also a good idea to group together herbs that require similar amounts of water or sun.

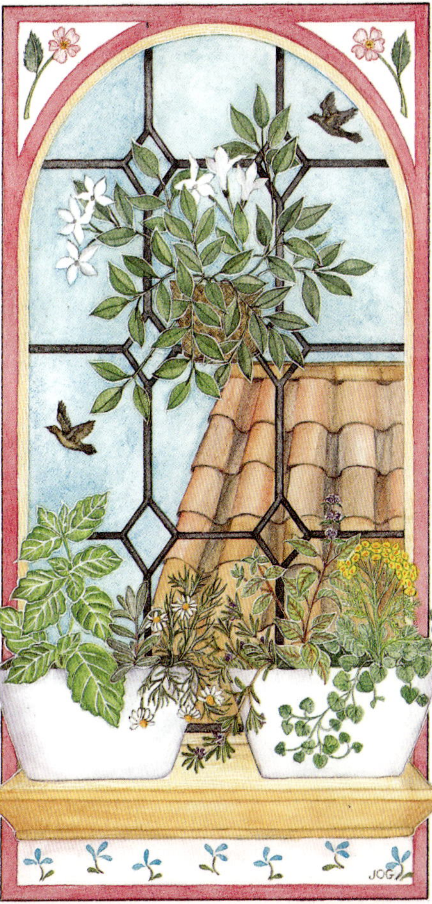
JOG

Groupings also can be made based on aesthetic considerations. For example, we can group herbs together by smell and color. In this way, we can enjoy the fresh smells of lavender intermixed with basil, or the beauty of purple-flowered sage juxtaposed with white-blossomed fennel.

We can also group herbs according to height. Lavender and rosemary, for example, make great hedges, while chamomile and thyme make an attractive ground cover.

When growing herbs outdoors, mulch should be added to reduce watering and weeds, and to protect plants from wind, storms, and both cold and heat. Indoors, we should ensure that plants get enough sunlight but not too much warmth. Ventilation is key as well: too little and our herbs become susceptible to insects and fungi.

Herbs that grow particularly well indoors include angelica, basil, bay, catnip, chamomile, dill, fennel, jasmine, mint, sage, tansy, and wintergreen.

Of course, we need not be gardeners to enjoy fresh herbs. Many can be gathered in the wild or even, in the case of herbs like dandelion and nettle, in our own backyards.

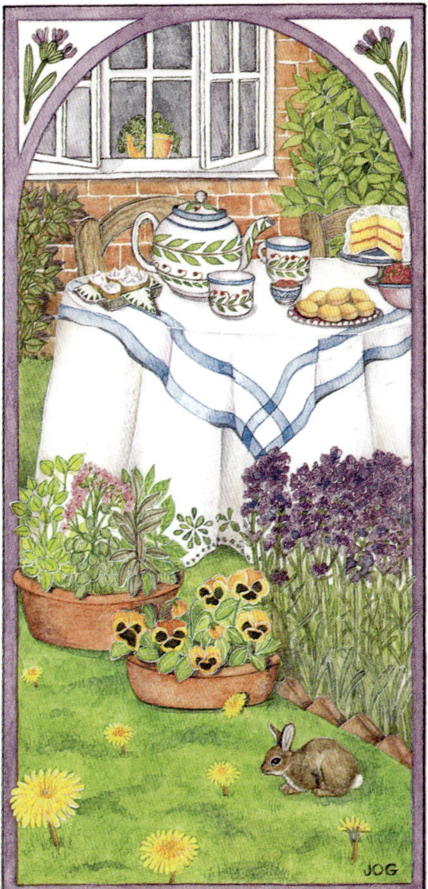
JOG

Harvesting the Rewards

Now that we've grown our herbs, it's time to harvest our bounty.

For a cup of tea "right off the vine," simply pinch off the tenderest leaves or gather tips of the plant's stalks rather than its full stem. This makes for the richest, most potent cup of tea possible.

We also can freeze or dry our herbs for later use. First, wash them thoroughly in cool water to remove all dirt and insects. Next, pat them dry with a paper towel. To freeze, simply place herbs whole or chopped in plastic bags or containers, and place in freezer.

To dry, we have three choices:

Microwave: Heat herbs on a low power for a minute or less (the exact time varies from oven to oven, herb to herb).

Conventional oven: Spread herbs on a rack and place in an oven set at 100–125 degrees F. Keep a watchful eye and the oven door open. The herbs take only moments to dry.

Air dry: In a dark, well-ventilated area, hang herbs upside down in bunches or on drying trays. To keep them dust-free, place them in paper bags with punched holes to let air in and moisture out. Drying time: a few days at the most.

Once dried, place herbs in air-tight containers or bags. Keep leaves, roots, and stems intact, to maintain their natural oils and flavors.

And what's the best way to brew a delicious cup of tea from our frozen or dried herbs? It's simple. Just add a cup of boiling water to about a teaspoon of the dried herb (or the defrosted frozen herb), steep for several minutes, then sip and enjoy!

Dessert Recipes to Accompany Herbal Teas

Meringue Nut Puffs

3 extra-large egg whites
3/4 cup confectioners sugar
1 teaspoon vanilla
1-1/4 cups finely chopped nuts

Preheat oven to 300° F. Line 2 cookie sheets with foil. Beat egg whites until stiff but not dry. Beat in sugar 2 tablespoons at a time. Fold in vanilla and nuts. Drop by tablespoonfuls, 2 inches apart, onto prepared cookie sheets. Bake about 35 minutes or until golden. Cool on cookie sheets. CAUTION: Don't make meringues in humid weather.

Makes about 3 dozen

Brandy Snaps

1/2 cup sweet butter
1/2 cup sugar
1/3 cup dark corn syrup
1 cup all-purpose flour
2-1/2 tablespoons brandy
1/2 teaspoon each: ginger, cinnamon, mace

Preheat oven to 375° F. Place butter, sugar, and corn syrup in saucepan over low heat. Cook until sugar is dissolved. Remove from heat and add flour slowly, stirring until smooth. Stir in remaining ingredients. Drop by 1/2 teaspoonfuls, 3 inches apart, onto ungreased cookie sheets. Bake 5 minutes until browned. Cool 3 minutes. Remove to racks and cool completely.

Makes about 2-1/2 dozen

Pound Cake

2 cups sweet butter
2 cups sugar
9 large eggs, separated
2 tablespoons orange juice
1 teaspoon vanilla
1/4 teaspoon salt
4-1/2 cups sifted cake flour

Preheat oven to 350° F. Grease and flour two 9 x 5 x 3-inch loaf pans. Cream butter and sugar in mixer until very light. Beat in egg yolks, one at a time. Beat in orange juice and vanilla. Add salt to sifted flour and sift again. Stir into butter mixture slowly. Beat egg whites to soft peak stage and fold into batter. Spoon into pans and bake 1 hour or until cake springs back when lightly pressed. Cool in pans 15 minutes. Remove from pans and cool completely on rack.

Makes about 18 servings

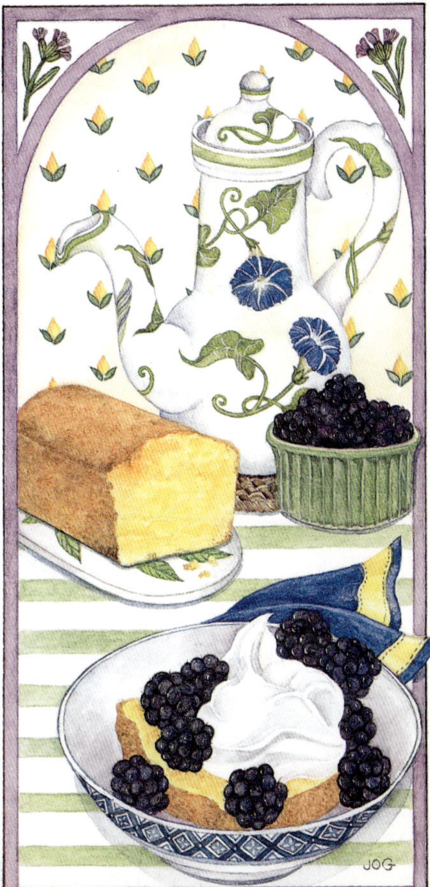
JOG

Chocolate Crispies

1/2 cup sweet butter
1 ounce unsweetened chocolate
1 egg, beaten
2/3 cup sugar
3/4 teaspoon vanilla
1/3 cup all-purpose flour
1/4 teaspoon salt
2/3 cup chopped nuts

Preheat oven to 375° F. Lightly grease 10 x 15-inch jelly-roll pan. Melt butter and chocolate in saucepan over low heat. Remove from heat and add egg very slowly, stirring constantly. Add sugar and vanilla. Stir well and fold in remaining ingredients. Spread evenly in prepared pan. Bake about 12 minutes until crisp. Cut into small squares immediately and remove from pan. Cool on racks.

Makes about 3 dozen

Mini Tea Cakes

1 cup sweet butter, room temperature
1/2 cup sugar
1 extra large egg, beaten
1 teaspoon vanilla
1/2 teaspoon salt
2 cups all-purpose flour
About 3 tablespoons jam

Preheat oven to 350° F. Cream butter and sugar in large bowl. Stir in egg and vanilla. Add salt to flour and stir into butter mixture gradually. Press about 1-1/2 tablespoons of dough into cups of ungreased miniature muffin pans. Smooth tops and make depression in center of each muffin. Fill each depression with about 1/4 teaspoon jam, using different kinds of jam, if desired. Bake 20 to 22 minutes. Cool in pans 10 minutes. Remove to racks and cool completely.

Makes about 3 dozen

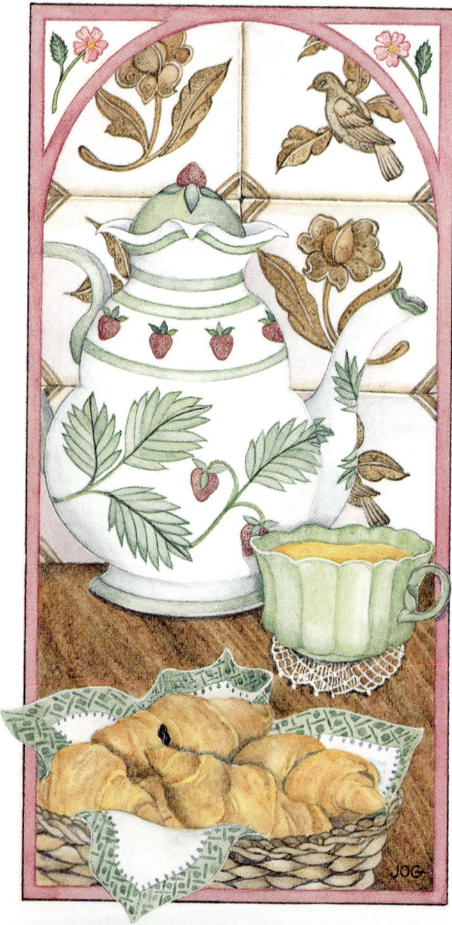
JOG

Filled Crescents

1/4 cup raisins
2 to 3 tablespoons orange juice
1 package (8 ounces) refrigerated crescents
1/4 cup brown sugar
Cinnamon
1/4 cup slivered almonds

Preheat oven to 375° F. Place raisins in cup and cover with orange juice. Let stand until raisins are plump. Unroll crescent dough on flat surface. Separate into 8 triangles. Drain raisins, discarding juice. Arrange raisins down center of each triangle and sprinkle with sugar, cinnamon, and almonds. Roll from widest side of triangle to opposite point and press point to seal. Place, point down, on ungreased cookie sheet and curve ends in to make crescent shapes. Bake about 12 minutes or until golden. Remove from cookie sheet.

Makes 8 crescents

Our Personal Tea Ceremony

*E*ven when we drink our tea alone, we're in good company. Many of the world's greatest thinkers–Confucius, Plato, Aristotle, to name just a few– enjoyed the delights of tea. And one wonders: How many of their great insights were shaped as they sat, pondered, and sipped?

Important insights await us as well, and what better way to draw them forth than with a cup of our favorite herbal tea in hand?

Let's create our own tea ceremony, then, one that allows us to sit quietly for 10 to 15 minutes a day and commune with ourselves. All we need is a favorite cup, a favorite tea, and a comfortable spot free of interruptions.

Holding our cup in our hands, close to our faces, let's close our eyes and take a few deep breaths. As we inhale the sweet aroma of our tea, let's enjoy its warmth and imagine that, with each exhalation, our troubles are leaving our bodies and minds.

As we relax, sip by sip, let's gently follow the path of our thoughts, taking care not to judge or direct them, but simply to note their presence. Or, we may choose to ask ourselves a single question–"What new direction can I take in my life?" for example, or "How can I have even more meaningful relationships with those I love?"–and then let our inner wisdom find the answer.

The Visual Beauty of Herbal Tea

*J*ust as we place crystals in our windows to cast rainbows on our walls, we can enjoy the lovely, natural bands of color that result when the sun filters through bottles of herbal tea.

First, we prepare a strong batch of a tea or blend whose color we find particularly appealing. Lavender flowers, for example, produce a soft purple hue, while hibiscus turn a deep, luscious red when steeped. Similarly, chamomile produces a sunny yellow, while chicory root produces rich shades of amber.

After the tea has brewed, carefully pour it into glass bottles that have lids or corks. Although any type of bottle or even drinking glass will do, the effect is enhanced by using decorative or antique bottles that are clear or slightly tinted.

Next, place these bottles in a window or on a shelf that gets direct sun for at least part of the day. Finally, sit back and let nature take its course, as the sun casts lovely bands of vibrant colors around the room.

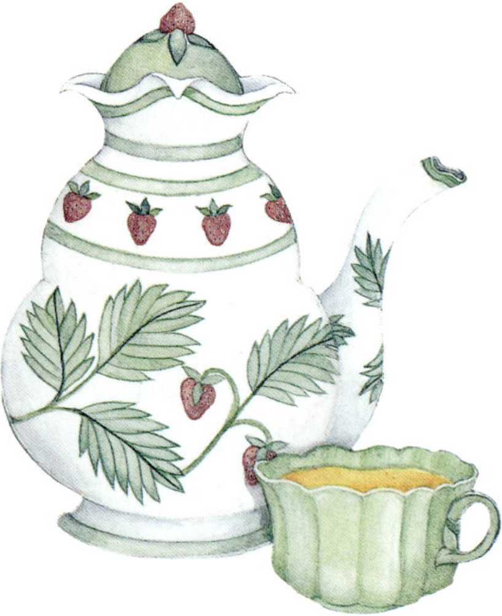